I0224201

LOW-HANGING FRUIT

poems by

Joanne Greenway

Finishing Line Press
Georgetown, Kentucky

LOW-HANGING FRUIT

ACKNOWLEDGMENTS

The poet wishes to extend her grateful acknowledgment to the publications
listed below which have published—or have accepted for publication—the
following poems:

"Postcard from Okemah, 1911," *For a Better World: Poems and Drawings on
Peace and Justice*, an anthology curated by Dr. Saad Ghosn, 2019
"Play On," Within Us, an anthology of the Greater Cincinnati Writers
League, brought to fruition by GCWL members Lynn Robbins and Mark
Lehman, 2020.
"Shouldda Been a Cowboy;"" "Watching My Father Weld," *Common Threads*,
Ohio Poetry Association
 "The Water Witch," *Pine Mountain Sand & Grave*l, No. 24, a journal of the
Southern Appalachian Writers Cooperative, 2021

Publisher: Leah Huete de Maines
Editor: Christen Kincaid
Cover Art: Joanne Greenway
Author Photo: Joanne Greenway
Cover Design: Elizabeth Maines McCleavy

Order online: www.finishinglinepress.com
also available on amazon.com

Author inquiries and mail orders:
Finishing Line Press
PO Box 1626
Georgetown, Kentucky 40324
USA

Table of Contents

SHOULDDA BEEN A COWBOY

Whenever Eddy Arnold's *Cattle Call* played
on the radio, you joined in on the yodeling.
Dad, how does a second generation Son of Italy
come by a love of hillbilly music? Perhaps
because you once walked behind a plow,
like Eddy Arnold, the "Tennessee plowboy."

If you could yodel, you were in a good mood.
On rainy days, your body and soul relived
the pain of blows you suffered as a child.
Yet, somehow, you still found a reason to sing.

You never missed an episode of *Gunsmoke*,
Rawhide or *Bonanza*—the Holy Trinity
of horse operas. If you were stepping out,
you'd don a fine, buff-colored Stetson
and western-style boots, raising your height
to a lofty five-foot five. People noticed.

Sure, behind your back, some folks snickered.
He ain't even Amurrican! Yet, here was this
sharp-dressed little guinea, playing cowboy.
You refused to hear them. All you heard
was Eddy Arnold, singing his cattle call,
with you on harmony vocal—two plowboys
yodeling until the cows came home.

CRACKER JACKED

Buy me some peanuts and Cracker Jack.
I don't care if I never get back.
"Take Me Out to the Ball Game"
—Lyrics by J. Norworth and A. Von Tilzer

Packaged in patriotic colors, America's
first junk food: Cracker Jack. Popcorn
and peanuts cloaked in caramel, so sweet
you could hear Mr. Tooth Decay at work.

Cracker Jack used to describe something
wonderful, like a crackerjack hunting dog.
Later, it implied cheap: *Cindy's engagement
ring must've come in a box of Cracker Jack.*

The box carried no warnings about choking
hazards or nut allergies, but each held a paltry
prize: a plastic ring or tin whistle. We kids
fought fiercely to claim the worthless booty.

To hell with postponing gratification—
we dumped the whole box into a bowl
instead of eating our way down to those
cheap little tchotchkes. Finders, keepers!

A staple at baseball games and a song lyric,
you can still buy Cracker Jack today.
Casualty of the digital age, the tiny buried
treasures have been replaced by a QR code.

Scan the code with your smart phone
to download the so-called prize, a silly
video game. I miss the lead-based charms,
fancy rings and little plastic farm animals.

Nowadays, the packaging has a new look:
Jack and his dog, Bingo, have had work done.
A hundred years later, only one thing remains
unchanged: Cracker Jack is still bad for you.

PICKING DROPS

We are kids, not professional pickers,
so trusted only to pick "drops," the ripe
apples that fall and collect on the ground,
before insects and dew turn them to rot.

Marti's dad pays us ten cents a crate.
Filling just one seems to take forever.
Wiry men and women on ladders pick
branches clean with long, brown fingers,
practiced at grabbing three or four apples
at a time with a near cartoonish speed.

In the late 1950s, all the pickers are Negro
migrant workers who travel up to New York
from Florida every fall in a procession
of battered cars. Some bring their children;
others leave them behind with grandparents.
The children attend local schools but learn
only how to endure playground cruelty.

At break time, we mix some grape Kool-Aid
and pass it around in paper cups. Marti
chases one of the migrant women and tries
to slip an ice cube down her shirt. Volina
returns the favor. Before long, we are all
chasing each other with ice cubes, slopping
Kool-Aid on our clothes. Stubborn purple
stains will test our mothers on wash day.
Today, there is no color in the orchard—
a level playing ground, ringing with laughter.

HARVEST

Barbara, do you remember how Larry
greeted you when you boarded the bus,
in his "mammy" voice? *Good mawnin',
sunshine.* Your dark skin betrayed no blush
of anger. Good mornings were rare for you,
the only Black girl in our school, a lone
brown raisin floating in a bowl of milk.

Do you remember another bad day on the bus
when Herbie jabbed you with a porcupine
quill in your backside? Instead of crying out,
you laughed giddily. Maybe too proud or
too scared to admit the prick had hurt you.

Neither of us will ever forget the one day
you did get angry—when Jimmy Grady
called you *nigger.*

Miss Pierce, the fourth grade teacher,
brokered the apology. We waited
in the hall, watching as she stood
over him, stern-faced. Doubtful
his remorse was genuine, you
had run out of cheeks to turn—
and forgave him anyway.

After the apple crop was in, all
the migrant families like yours
moved on. There were other crops
to pick, in other states, and a new
crop of kids to taunt and tease you.

One more growing season.
One more harvest of hurt.

POSTCARD FROM OKEMAH, 1911

Laura and L.D. Nelson, a Black mother and son, were lynched
near Okemah, Oklahoma, on May 24, 1911.

Lynching made murder into a social event,
not unlike a square dance, picnic or barbecue—
large crowds would gather to watch. People
brought their children and hampers of food:
cold roast chicken, corn bread—and cruelty.

In the photo, you can almost hear the hum
of the all-white crowd along the bridge,
baking in the glower of a mid-day sun.
Above them, a Black woman hangs,
limp and still as a rag doll. No breeze ruffles
the folds of her dress. A few yards away
hangs her son. Their assassins left them
strung up from the bridge rail—the way
hunters will do with a quarry of game birds.

Condemned without trial for theft of a cow
and murder of a deputy, their hanged corpses
were photographed, and the image made
into grisly picture postcards.

Decades later, a troubadour will learn
his own daddy had taken part in the crime.
In wishful song lyrics, he claims the cries
of their victims robbed the murderers
of sleep for the rest of their lives.

The gawkers lining the bridge—men,
women, even children—stare blankly
into the camera. I search their faces
in vain for a single furtive tear, proof
that someone felt something like shame.

The image of those bodies, hanging high
above the river, broken and defiled, clings
to my mind, impossible to un-see. They
were buried in shallow, unmarked graves.
Lives erased, bones beaten to dust.

Dust borne off by the Sooner wind.

MAKING GRAPE JELLY

I am too little to help, but I love
watching my mother make jelly
from a bursting basket of grapes,
deep purple, iridescent with bloom.

The path from produce to product
is involved: wash, stem and crush
the fruit in the big graniteware pot.
Boil, then simmer to an ink-dark
pulp. The kitchen and my lungs fill
with the warm, wine-scented steam.

Tiny beads of perspiration assemble
on Ma's forehead and upper lip. I worry
about burns as she strains the scalding
hot juice to separate out the skins
and seeds, returning it to simmer
again with six cups of sugar and
the crucial congealer, pectin.

Into the waiting jars, some clear,
some blue-green, she pours the hot
liquid. Once the jellies firm up, she
ladles melted paraffin over them,
fastens lids. Stored in the fridge,
they keep for about two months.

I get tiny bits of wax in my teeth
whenever I open a fresh jar; a small
price to pay for the sugary, syrupy
sludge that made Skippy sing out loud
and sat like sunshine on my tongue.

WATCHING MY FATHER WELD

Vulcan must have had a hand
in my father's talent for fender
and body work, so skilled at welding,
the undisputed Bernini of the torch.

I stand at a safe distance, while my father
dons gloves, coveralls and welder's hood,
all black, sinister-looking. Laser-focused,
he moves his torch deftly along a seam,

the metal bead melting gold, green
and blue, into the parent metal,
sluicing like butter, spreading to join
the pipe sections perfectly. Lightning-like

flashes, showers of sparks, like fireflies
that spangle our dark summer skies.
So much to learn from this process:
the dignity of working with one's hands,

the importance of getting things right
the first time, respect for the vagaries
of metal, its tolerance for bending
and bonding, its tensile strength.

All qualities to be admired in a man
who penetrated the mysteries of his
material and shaped it to his will.

When he tried it with his daughter,
he learned I was not made of metal.

THE WATER WITCH

*Martin Luther condemned divination an act of heresy, but
St. Theresa of Avila built her convent where a dowser had found water.*

Sam Horn churned up a cloud of dust,
his old beater lurching up the dirt lane.
A small crowd had gathered, eager to see
if a man could find water with a stick.

Along for the ride, a trunk-load of dowsing rods:
peach, willow and hazel-wood. For this job,
he chose the hazel-wood. My father had
rarely drilled a dry hole. If he was skeptical,
he was curious, too—it was a drought year.

Over his short-sleeved shirt, Sam wore
a catcher's chest protector. As he paced
the property, my brother Bo and I trailed
him until he stopped short and lurched
wildly, staggering to keep his feet—
engaged in a tug-of-war with a demon.

The forked branch then suddenly jerked
ground-ward. *Plant the stake right there,
at the tip o' my foot*, he instructed Bo.
Eyes closed, face tilted skyward, the twig
tapped out on his padded chest how deep
the water lay. The unforgiving July sun
beat down; his shirt darkened with sweat.

This spectacle repeated several times.
Was he a charlatan or was there some
spiritual connection between man and
element? Scientists insist the rods'
movement is an "ideomotor response,"
not due to some hidden agent. No more
believable than alchemy or astrology.

Bo has been a driller—and a water witch,
for over sixty years. Instead of a branch,
he uses two bent brass rods. When he walks
over a vein, he swears the rods move, outward.

My brother is a Pisces—he always finds water.

VENUS SPEAKS

I was her favorite—fast and spook-proof—
an equine version of her. Named me Venus,
for the Greek goddess of Love and Victory.
A fearless rider, Belle knew how to sit a horse.

Straight-backed and queenly, she rode me
sidesaddle. Wore a black velvet riding habit,
a feather-trimmed hat and two Colt .45s.
Belle always looked good on my back.

On his Missouri farm, her father raised blooded
horses. She grew to love them more than her own
kin. Once punished her son for mistreating me
with several searing strokes of the bull whip.

Reputed to be a crack shot, some swore Belle
could hit a piece of paper sideways. It was
the Civil War what ruined everything for her.
It was either sell her ass, starve or steal horses.

Belle—French for beautiful—she was not.
She was married three times, widowed twice.
Jim Reed: shot. Sam Starr: shot. Only Jim July,
young enough to be her son, would outlive her.

Riding me home one day after lunch with friends,
her bosom still dusted with cornbread crumbs,
Belle was blown out of my saddle by a single
shotgun blast—a crime unsolved to this day.

Carved on her tombstone, the image
of a strong, sturdy horse and this epitaph:

> *Shed not for her the bitter tear,*
> *Nor give the heart to vain regret.*
> *'Tis but the casket that lies here,*
> *The gem that filled it sparkles yet.*

And that horse? I like to think it's me.

BILL WAS A LOVER—AND A LIBBER

In his photos, he is the cowboy archetype,
courtesy of central casting: handsome and lean,
shoulder-length mane, all beads, buckskin
and fringe. A man's man. A lady's man.

As fond as he was of real women, Bill cherished
"Lucretia Borgia," his buffalo rifle, above all.
A Springfield .50 caliber trapdoor needle gun,
she was, like her 15th century namesake, deadly.

Louisa Frederici, a fiery, Tuscan beauty
was his only wife, but their fifty-year union
was as rocky and rutted as a wagon trail,
full of strife, separations and suspicion.

A handsome man, away from the marital bed
for long stretches, he was surely tempted
to kick over the traces. Attractive women
threw themselves at him constantly. There is
little doubt he had caught some of them.

When he formed *Buffalo Bill's Wild West*,
Annie Oakley was its biggest draw,
demonstrating shooting skill that left
menfolk dumbfounded. Where did he find
this wiry hillbilly gal who never missed?

Once, on learning Susan B. Anthony
was in the stands, he galloped his horse
up to her box. Jaws dropped when he doffed
his hat, bowed low, brushing his beard
against the saddle horn—a shocking act.

Larger than life Bill Cody was—but Death
came calling and got the drop on him.
On his tombstone, these spare sentiments:

> *Noted scout and Indian fighter.*

I'd add another line for a man who lived
fast and loved hard his whole life long:

> *He prized all women—he knew their worth.*

FIRST COMMUNION

It's a welcome-to-the faith gift, a handbag
filled with items any new little bride of Christ
could possibly covet. Among the treasures
in my "starter kit": a Catholic prayer book,
with gilt-edge pages; a lace chapel veil;
rosary beads, fashioned of seed pearls,
and a deck of junior saints cards, including
St. Joan, my name saint—the one who
heard voices, cross-dressed and led
an army. My kind of saint. But branded
a heretic, she went up in holy smoke.

Lastly, there were a pair of scapular medals,
postage stamp-sized, strung on a cord. You
wore these under your clothes, one medal
in front, one in back, the Catholic answer
to Mormon underwear. If I died wearing them
I'd be spared the fires of eternal damnation—
but I'd still be dead. I was not religious
about wearing the medals—or much else.
Mine were drowned and mutilated
in my mother's wringer washer.

On the big day, I donned my meringue
dress and knelt at the communion rail.
The wafer tasted like paper and stuck
to the roof of my mouth. It was nothing
like a 'Nilla Wafer. We were told to swallow,
not chew the Body of Christ, so it remained
stuck 'til breakfast. I asked Father if they
came in other flavors like, say, chocolate.

My mother, curdled at my gaffe, blamed it
on hunger from fasting—"mortification
of the flesh." Father, suppressing a smile,
was calculating my penance for blasphemy.
A new record for elapsed time from sacrament
to sacrilege. Mommy's little cross to bear.

JESUS WEPT

Friends with pure intentions shepherd me,
newly widowed, to their church to receive
"gifts of the Spirit." I haven't the heart to tell
them I'm an atheist—like my late husband.

The Temple of Abundant Life used to be a home
to someone. Sun floods the chapel through windows
covered with stained glass patterned Con-Tact paper.
Achingly clean, a faint odor of lemon lingers.

As instructed, I wear a modest skirt. I will fake
piety, just for today. I hum through their hymns.
Some of the faithful form a line at the mic,
to testify how the Savior has saved them.

In a sudden shift of tone, a red-faced deacon,
radiant with rage, slams a homily of homophobia.
I am stunned to discover hate has a home
in this house of God—as do bosh and bull.

A young woman with a halo of golden hair
steps up, Bible in hand, she opens her throat
and speaks, but not in the words of man.
Brimming with the Holy Spirit, she erupts

in a torrent of incoherent words, so rapid-fire,
they fade before I can get any sense of them:
*Kolama siándo, ama conda amus. Keamo
deamo no ma diamos. Kelalaiyanano.*

I don't know what Jesus would do. I want
to stand up and scream at these sheep. This
is not how you get closer to God! If I were
a praying sort, I'd pray for them to reject
sham and showmanship, embrace tolerance
and truth. In my stem-winder sermon, I'd urge
them to live their Christianity every day,
not just for this one-hour Sunday side show.

*People, choose faith over dogma and doggerel.
Satan is not a snake! Women, put on some pants!*

HAPPY MEAL

The cleanest table I find in McDonald's
is cater-cornered from a woman and
two children. I squirm in my molded
plastic seat when my gaze settles
on the children, suppressing an urge
to gasp. Their little mugs are melted
in places. Their scorched scalps
are puzzles. Patches of hair, patches
of stone-smooth skin—where hair
will never grow again. I want to find
the missing pieces, reassemble them.

I avoid staring, then wonder how
they might feel if I turn away.
When we do make eye contact,
I smile and hope it looks sincere.
Heedless of my angst, and a future
filled with skin grafts and suffering,
they tuck into their cheeseburgers,
happy with their Happy Meals.

I ponder the mossy cliché and pray
them a beauty deeper than skin-deep.

AMOSANDRA

In the photo, a four year-old me sits next to cousin
Anita, on the trunk of a sappy fallen fir. A powerful
storm had brought it down onto our old house,
taking a bite out of the roof. In my lap, I clutch
my naked, one-armed doll. A special dolly.
No other little girl I knew had one like her.

The Amosandra doll was named after the baby girl
born to Ruby and Amos on the old *Amos 'n' Andy*
radio show, a portmanteau for the male leads, Black
men played by white actors, speaking in minstrelsy
dialect. Only when the show moved to television
were Black actors hired to play those parts.

Save for her cocoa skin, Amosandra seemed cast
from the same mold as any white doll. Neither
her hair nor face were those of a real little Black girl.
I loved her to pieces—which may have cost her
that arm. Even so, she could still drink from a bottle,
wet her diaper and, when squeezed, cry for me.

Decades later, I meet her again as I surf eBay.
A wave of nostalgia leaves me unmoored
and close to tears when I happen upon
a vintage Amosandra in her original box.

Doll, clothing and accessories: three hundred bucks.
I do not click "Add to cart." I leave her in the past.
My beloved doll gave the lie to a color-blind
playground that never was—and is yet to be.

MY LITTLE FRIEND

City People poured into our hamlet every July
and August, filling rental homes and bungalows.
Mostly Italian-Americans from the Bronx, they
had lots of children. At last, I had playmates.

I didn't get along with some of the girls
who seemed bossy and smarter than me—
like the vaguely menacing, dark-eyed Amelia
who took command of our play sessions,

who even "borrowed" my new doll—the one
with the pink taffeta dress and combable hair—
to show her mother. I begged for its return.
Amelia kept stalling. Every Sunday, at Mass,

I'd see her at the communion rail, serenely taking
the wafer while my dolly languished captive
in her frilly bedroom. Surely, her mother
noticed a new doll among Amelia's collection.

My own mother asked what had become of her.
I lied and told her I'd lost "Tosca." Years later,
Mom told me Amelia's Daddy was a soldier—
not in the army, but in a New York crime family.

He'd murdered a Black youth, witness to a mob
hit. The young man's body was dumped
into the Hudson. I 'fessed up about the doll.
My mother was relieved I had not lost it—

and that I knew how to pick my fights.

LA PENSIONE D'ALL INFERNO
(The Pensione from Hell)

It's 1968. Three thousand lira will buy a bed
for the night and a continental breakfast.
Bare bones, no pool, no TV, not even a fan
to counter the Eternal City's infernal heat.

A bearded youth wearing a Yale tee shirt
greets me at the desk. Smiling and lying
through his dingy, picket fence teeth,
he swears to a working toilet and hot water.

I struggle up worn marble stairs, lugging
my outlandish, over-packed pink suitcase.
The door to my room does not lock. The toilet
flushes only occasionally. The hot water?

Unreliable. Still, Pensione Aedes has its charms:
ornate cornices, carved woodwork and a campanile,
silent for want of a bell. From a distance, she is
a beautiful woman who has known hard times.

In the morning, the hot water disappears
mid-shampoo. After a heated argument
laced with the few Italian insults I know,
I agree to pay half, then leave in a huff.

My still-wet head dries in the Roman sun
on my way to better lodgings. Senora Pacelli,
Italian career widow, robed head-to-toe
in black, shows me to my pristine, room.

La Senora hands me the keys then heads
to a weeknight Mass. The room smells
faintly of bleach and the bed linens feel
like cardboard against my skin. In two weeks,

I'll be flying home. Home, where my own bed
waits, made up with line-dried percale sheets.

THE "FORGET-YOU" HOLE

1968, my summer abroad, my French hosts
take me on a road trip around the Val de Loire.
Our itinerary includes Saché, where Balzac
filled up on coffee while filling the pages
of his novels filleting the privileged class.

Next stop: the Château de Chinon where
we chance upon one of the *fifilles*—
a pet name for the *oubliette*. From the verb
oublier, to forget, a thirty-foot deep
hole where the king's enemies were dumped
and forgotten—left to rot until they died
or were released—if ever. The *gentille
Ministre de la Culture*, for visitors' safety,
has installed an iron grate over it.

Still, I watch my step. I cannot un-see
the nightmarish descent into darkness
from which there would be no escape.
Below my feet, agony and oblivion.
All round me a day so peaceful and rare,
I cling to it like a precious jewel

that could be lost forever if, in one
careless moment, I loosen my grip.

COLOSSUS IN THE CORN BELT

Ohio, home of the weird, you boast a museum
of swallowed objects in Lima, a Cornhenge
in Columbus, a pencil sharpener museum in Logan.

But the jewel in your crown was the yellow,
sixty-foot-tall steel and Styrofoam Jesus,
standing in a man-made lake, arms upraised,
in front of the Solid Rock Church in Monroe.

Since its erection in 2006, Jesus's outsized likeness
stood facing I-75, impossible to miss in either direction.
Officially known as King of Kings, his pose
and complexion earned him many mocking
monikers—Touchdown Jesus, Big Butter Jesus.

Flash forward to June, 2010, and a storm of Biblical
proportions. From out of the firmament, a bolt
of lightning strikes Him, turning Touchdown Jesus
into a toxic torch, a charred skeleton. The bitterest
irony of all—our Savior could not be saved.

In two years' time, a new colossus supplants
him. The *Lux Mundi* Jesus is shorter by ten feet,
the pose less passionate. Wearing the same
creamed corn complexion, he stands atop a pile
of rocks with open arms, beseeching a hug.

A short drive south, a throng of cast cement giraffes
welcomes hoarders to Trader's World, a mega flea market.
Jesus and the Almighty Buck, separated by a mere
mile of macadam, compete for the same idolaters.

COUNTING CARS

Slow means full, fast means empty. Train
whistle blasts, one long, two short, rouse
memories decades old. I'm a child again,
bouncing in the back seat of a '47 Chevy,

waiting for a long freight train to pass.
We wave to the brawny engineer and
he waves back. They always do. He
is hauling a mile's worth of steel,

more than a hundred cars. When the red
caboose finally passes, we shout and
send it off in a chorus of our loudest,
most convincing train whistle hoots.

Today, from my hillside perch, I watch a freight
train crawl across a rusted trestle high above
the mighty Ohio, a graffiti-riddled shank
slicing through Cincinnati's heart.

Southern Pacific, CSX, Santa Fe, BNSF,
all pulling boxcars, flatcars, hoppers,
tank cars and covered wagons, carrying
coal, light trucks, iron ore and fuel oil.

Track maintenance is automated now,
gone are the gandy dancers. Gone, too,
the brakeman and caboose, replaced
by a Digital Era "end-of-train" device.

As the train disappears, I whistle a soft
dirge—one long, two short blows.

HOUSEWORK EPIPHANY
a Villanelle

"Cleanliness is, indeed, next to godliness."
—John Wesley, ca 1791

I meant to do a thousand things today,
but I've had a fall, a slow, scary descent.
I do not bounce well, so where I land, I stay.

Best to rest as I lie here, in pain and disarray,
studying clots of dust in the ceiling vent.
I swear to do a thorough cleaning someday.

Can't find my feet, struggle though I may,
I am pinned under my ladder, stunned and bent.
I do not bounce well, so where I land, I stay.

Gripped by my worst fear, will I lie here all day,
beneath the gunked-up dust on the ceiling vent?
I vow to do a deep, detailed cleaning someday.

I struggle to rise, to rejoin the daily fray.
To fly and rule the sky, that is my intent—
after I do a careful cleaning today.

The trees have shed all their leaves, to my dismay.
Like me, where the leaves land, they stay, still and spent.
Lying inert, they meld with the dirt and decay…
Godliness? Sounds like something a man would say.

COCA COLA FIREWORKS

In our fly speck town, folks mark
the end of World War Two
as if it's the last we'll ever fight.
They celebrate, not with a parade
or other patriotic display of flags
and fireworks. The men in my family
will improvise their own spectacle.

An army bus drops my soldier uncle
off across the street, his arm in a sling.
Four campaigns in the Pacific theater
have earned him a purple heart with clusters.
Shell-shock will last him the rest of his life.

Cousin Louise, with her staunch right arm,
launches empty Coke bottles high in the air.
My father shoots them all out of the sky,
one after the other. Starbursts of green glass
dazzle the spectators gathered, mouths agape.

My brother, cap-guns strapped to his waist,
cheers each hit, near manic with joy.
Daddy shoot the gun! No more war!
All of them, so in thrall to victory, they cannot
imagine the lost wars and lives still ahead,
in Korea, Vietnam, Iraq… Afghanistan.

These days, war thrives, relentless. Peace
is rare—like Coke in green glass bottles.

AUNT MARGIE'S DOLCE VITA

A chatterbox, scatter-brained Betty Boop—
headful of black curls, red bow lips,
eternally haloed in cigarette smoke,
bright toothbrush smile—my Aunt Margie.

Wed to a World War Two vet, theirs was
a marriage made in Akron. Between bouts
of bickering, they'd take over any dance
floor and jitterbug 'til the band stopped playing.

Though not the brightest crayon in the box,
she started her own business, making pastries.
No food handler's license? No problem. She
supplied thousands of contraband cannoli

to local restaurants, singing 1950s Hit Parade
songs while she rolled and shaped the dough.
Her untrained voice was good enough to land
her fifteen minutes of fame on *Name That Tune*.

The big money prize eluded her, but she nailed
the tune when the band played the first four notes
of *Come on-a My House*, a Romanian folksong
sung in a phony Italian accent, a monster hit

for Rosemary Clooney. Smoking and singing
her way through packs of Lucky Strikes, Aunt Margie
could sing the entire Clooney songbook and weather
every storm of life. Long gone now, I know she

is still singing somewhere. There's an earworm
playing in my head of Aunt Margie baking
and belting those looney Clooney lyrics:

Come on-a my house, a my house,
I'm gonna give-a you candy...

What she gave-a *me* was a crisp pastry tube
filled with a sweetened ricotta cream. I was
powerless against it. When a clueless friend
suggested she make a low-fat version,

without missing a beat, she snapped: *Girl,*
do ya make love with your panties on?

WHAT MRS. PELL TAUGHT ME

Our Home Ec. teacher wore her honey hair
in a beehive, shellacked into submission
with Aqua Net. Her fashion statement:
a smooth shirtwaist, prim Peter Pan collar.

Baking is chemistry! Tamper with a cake
recipe and failure awaits. Read your recipe.
girls. Measure all ingredients beforehand,
what the French call a *mise en place.*

Sew your own school wardrobe! I made
a skirt out of dirt-brown cotton duck
from a McCall's pattern. So ugly, I wore
it to school once—just for her to see.

Children are a gift from God! Raise them
with love and limits. Praise and prayer
work better than paddling. Reward
good behavior with a sugar cookie.

At age 41, she quit teaching when God
finally blessed the Pells with a dimpled demon
babysitters dubbed "Kyle, the Wild Chile,"
a Terrible Two well into adulthood.

One night, he and two of his buddies dropped
a fifty-pound rock from a Thruway overpass
and killed a 22 year-old woman. A joke, he told
the judge. Twenty years, said the judge, no joke.

Years later, our carts intersect at a Shop Rite.
She knows I know. Eyes shining with tears,
she rues her late motherhood. *I did everything
right: Sunday school, pre-school, den mother, PTA...*

And I baked all those goddamned cookies.

ALL AMERICAN BOY

Jerry was the smartest kid in the Class of '58—
a GPA of four-point-O, near perfect SAT
scores, National Honor Society, Eagle Scout,
and Rifle club, too. Our English teacher said
one day, we'd read about him in the papers,
or see him on TV. Jerry had forged a clear path:
ROTC, West Point—a stellar military career.

Spit-and-polish in appearance, his mother
pressed his shirts to perfection, ironed razor-sharp
creases in his khakis. To complete the look,
he wore his auburn-tinged hair in a brush cut.
People joked about his ramrod straight posture.
That Jerry walks like he's got a stick up his ass.
Whip-smart and confident, who had a better right
to walk head-high, like a brigadier general?

One spring night, while his parents watched TV
in their paneled den, Jerry repaired to his room.
Homework, he said. Quietly, he sat down
and loaded his rifle. Then tied one end
of a rawhide bootlace to his big toe, the other
to the trigger. Such a considerate son, he had
placed some plastic sheeting on the floor.

The single shot tore through his brain. In his note,
he apologized to his family. *I'm tired of living
in this rat race.* We were dumbfounded. If life
was a race, Jerry was most likely to win it.
What made him want to give up? By age seventeen,
he was running on fumes, and we were clueless.

It's so hard to see clearly in a blinding light.

SELF-QUARANTINE LAMENT

Memories of the coronavirus lockdown, 2020-2021.

Corona-imposed cabin fever has me
missing much of what I used to curse.

Flesh-on-flesh could cure my touch
hunger. I even miss the suspect pats
from touchy-feely Joe the Doorman.

I would welcome the sun on my face,
even if it burns me. Even learn to love
the smell of car exhaust as much as
new-mown grass. Obnoxious children,
where the hell are you? I miss your
ear-splitting schoolyard shrieks.

Flowering trees, what I wouldn't give
to clean your green pollen off my car
again. Magnolias, I want to hug you,
feel your fleshy flowers. Vexing
vectors, like mosquitos, continue
to maintain your social distance.

I live to hear once more you buzzing
bees though your sting can turn my skin
into a pebbly mass. My allergies aside,
I would sacrifice my tender hide
for you—and for the flowers' sake.

THE CIDADA SPEAKS
Thousands and thousands of cicadas visited us in 2021.

It's a tedious cycle: we tunnel our way
to the surface, dive-bomb any human
who gets in the way and cover every tree
with our eggs. Many of us will suffer
predation: insecticides, birds, cats
and badminton racquets. We cannot escape
every angry footfall, but we will live long
enough to see thousands of our progeny
emerge. Only to eat and burrow back
underground to start the cycle yet again.

Take notice of our lacy green wings,
bulbous orange bug eyes. Hear our
relentless whine on hot summer days—
a male chorus loud enough to fill
every human head with an incessant,
insect monotone, rising and falling
in volume. Surrender to it as you drowse
and dream in your rope hammock.

With every generation comes a promise
of a ten-fold increase in population.
Do the math. You are outnumbered.
We are inescapable—for a while.
Just like Death. When you finally
follow us underground, you will not
leave behind delicate brown shells
clinging to trees and leaves—
and you will not be invited back.

THE LAST CHICKEN

After the war, Dad sold most of his acreage
to my uncle. All that remained of the family
farm were a dying orchard, a chicken coop
and its last tenant, a puny white pullet.

Shrieking desperately as she fled my father
and his upraised axe, she was soon cornered,
beheaded and left to bleed out in the kitchen
sink, prepped for plucking and gutting.

My mother made her into a delicious
pollo alla cacciatora, enrobing her
in a rich tomato sauce. I struggled
to swallow with a throatful of guilt.

Accustomed to seeing her every day
pecking jerkily about the yard, it seemed
a betrayal to eat her. The loop of her
last frenzied moments haunted me.

When Death was near; she knew enough
to run for her life. They always know.

LOSING GROUND

A 700-mile slog via Interstate 80 has become
my *hegira*. The endless macadam ribbon takes
this country mouse back to the theater where I
played out the first act of my life. A place

of gentle hills—and quirky farm folk plucked
from a Grant Wood painting. In the before times,
my corner of the Mid-Hud was a picture postcard,
edged by the pewter grey ribbon of the Hudson

on one side, and the stooped shoulders
of the Shawangunk range on the other, near
the site of Rip van Winkle's infamous hangover.
A child version of me once roamed open fields,

gathered wildflowers, climbed apples trees,
scooped tadpoles from roadside streams, fed
Mr. Biaggi's goats. Knew all the neighbors,
the names of their children—even their dogs.

Demographic Shift moved in with stealth.
Manhattanites, fleeing the noise, crime, and
inflated rents—bought up land and houses.
McMansions mushroomed where Holsteins

once grazed. Vineyards have overtaken orchards
and corn fields. There's a wine-tasting trail
—the big tourist draw in the fall. Chardonnay
and rosé supplanted beer and apple cider.

City kids hunker down over their iPads. They
don't chase lightning bugs on dark summer nights,
they freak when baby goats suckle their fingers—
and they can't tell jewelweed from poison ivy.

ALUMNI NEWSLETTER

As I scan the *In Memoriam* page, my gaze
rivets on a familiar name. Dreamboat Pete,
who sat next to me in music class, has died.
My older man college crush was no more.

Vital and vigorous—surely not old enough
to die. Then I remembered his fondness
for cigarettes. Sexy, square-jawed Pete,
had dimples that could catch rainwater.

He smelled good, too. English Leather!
I was a French major and impressed him
with my pronunciation of *L'Apres-midi
d'un Faun* and *Le Carnaval des Animaux*.

The first time he sat down next to me,
he offered me a stick of gum. I reacted
like he was a Yank GI liberating Paris
and I a starving *gamine*, ready to trade

my virtue for a Hershey Bar and nylons.
The irksome reality: he was married.
Unavailable—and too old for me.
Still, I hiked up my skirt a bit more

each week in an attempt to seduce him
in *Music 101*. Pete's face in my space
was a thrill twice a week. What did I
care about Chopin, Debussy or Satie?

Even now, my knees still turn to jelly
at the sight of a pack of Juicy Fruit.

MOVING DAY

The experts warn, never fall in love
with a house. I fell hard for this one.
A coup de foudre fairytale castle
from story books mother read me:
white-painted brick, spiral staircase,
even a turret and cottage garden.
The living room was big enough
for a baby grand. My Piano Man
and I had found our happy ever after.

Until, one day, the wicked witch Cancer
poisoned the Prince, leaving me to rattle
around in this house like a marble in a maze.
I said I'd never leave—you'd have to carry
me out feet-first. Now, the rooms are
piled with cardboard boxes, packed
with the artifacts of my life. I will move
myself and my goods to a charmless
glass and granite condo. Before I leave,
I press my face against the cool plaster
walls and bid farewell to my beloved home.

I hear piano music in the hall and stairwell.
Am I hearing things? No. It's Piano Man,
playing a Johnny Mercer standard on the baby
grand. I pour myself a glass of Merlot.

> *We're drinking my friend, to the end*
> *Of a brief episode*
> *Make it one for my baby*
> *And one more for the road*

All through the house, memories reach out,
pull at my sleeve, imploring me to stay.
Until I hear a stage whisper in my ear…

Just go.

PLAY ON

I am invisible. This superpower
is a dubious perk of widowhood.
Waiting for a table at a restaurant,
the hostess will ask, *Are we dining
alone today, dear?* Why, yes, we are.

Friends stop calling three weeks
after the service. I fill my days
shopping, volunteering and sorting
through the mail that still comes
for him. *LAST CHANCE! Renew
your subscription to PC World now!*
I reply on a Post-it Note: *Sorry.
Both my husband and his PC
crashed at about the same time.*

Some mornings, I awake and forget
he is gone. Dream hangover. I bring
him back with a CD of Chick Corea
on keyboards, vocals by Flora Purim.

> *Some time ago, I had a dream.
> It was happy, it was laughing,
> it was free.*

Issues of *PC World* will continue
for another six months, my grief
will go on. When I start to wallow,
I hear him urging me, in the lingo
of improv jazz, *Get your licks in.
No more comping. Learn to solo.*

THERAPY DOG

No over-sized lap dog, he.
Never cuddly. Perpetual motion,
hard to hold. The tail wagged
the dog when he got excited—
think Robin Williams in a dog suit.
Counter-surfer, sock-stealer,
defiler of flowerbeds, he was
a one-dog wrecking crew.

Never keen to lick my face
or snuggle next to me on the sofa,
a brawling "tough guy" Airedale.
Fierce defender, it didn't matter
if the intruder was a church lady
dropping off a batch of cookies
or an invading army, his response
was the same—a booming bark,
a menacing mug in the window,
white teeth flashing like sabers.
Meter readers skipped my house.
Jehovah's Witnesses, too.

Only once in all his dog years
did he display his softer side.
When Old Man died and left
me all alone, that first night,
unbidden, he jumped onto the bed
and spooned with me 'til morning.

One leap, one loving gesture,
kept my broken heart alive.

HEARTBREAK AT WHOLE FOODS

Maybe he can't read—or can't count.
The sign says, TEN ITEMS OR LESS.
In open defiance of supermarket protocol,
he cuts in front of me in the Express Lane.

At once, his motives become clear.
The redheaded vixen at Register 5 has him
hypnotized. Ringing up Romeo's pricey
provisions, she ignores his very small talk.

Prince Charming pulls out his best pick-up
lines, fails to engage. She scans and bags,
enduring his not quite rapier wit. While he
dallies, I can almost hear my arches falling.

In a last ditch effort to con a date, he slides
his business card across the counter to her.
He is wasting his time. *No way you'll
ever bag her, pal.* Yet, he lingers!

My aching back cries out for justice. I bump
his ass with my cart. I barely beg his pardon.
He's still within earshot when I rasp,
Ms. Hottie's out of your league, lover-boy.

A smile wrinkles her perfect little nose.
The dam breaks; she spills a waterfall of giggles.

Let her laugh. Her market is thronged today;
how many will come tomorrow?

SHOP 'TIL YOU DROP

"So, where to, ma'am?"

Without missing a beat, she tells me:
Brooks Brothers, on Fountain Square.

"Looking to drop a lot of cash, are we?

*I am done looking for bargains. If this
is my last Christmas, Ben's gift needs
to be something that will outlive me.*

"Christ, you're so morbid. What happened
to your faith in God? In Medicine?
Not necessarily in that order."

*So far, no miracles, no signs from God.
At this point, my doctors are playing for pride.*

From a rack, she pulls a forty-five dollar silk tie.
"For that money, you could buy him two dress shirts
at Sear's," I remind my suddenly spendthrift friend.

*It's only money. Remember when I used to recycle
aluminum foil? By the time this charge shows up
on my Visa, I'll be composting in some cemetery.*

"You've decided to give up."

*After the second kid, remember how I wanted a tummy
tuck? Now, I'm down forty pounds and shedding
faster than a Persian cat. I can't stand the sight of me.
I want to drape all the mirrors in the house with bedsheets.
I don't make plans. I don't even buy green bananas.*

"You're just tired."

*I'm tired of fighting. Tired of all the cheerleading:
Rickety-rackety, rickety-razz!
I'm gonna kick cancer's ass!*

The problem is, everyone expects me to get well.

LOW-HANGING FRUIT

Our religious instruction teacher was
a pale, powdered husk of a woman.

Mrs. Hinkleman held her blue eyes
wide open, like a woman cornered
by a serial killer—waiting for the axe.

If she had a mission statement, it was
to mold us into good Catholic girls
with a sense of sin and shame—and
an abundance of scare tactics. Love God,
by all means—but fear Him, because
The Devil is everywhere, girls—setting
traps to lead you into temptation!

One thing she made very clear: we
should not touch our bodies—or let boys
take liberties with our person. Never mind
we were still in third grade and had no idea
what the hell she was talking about.

Only good girls get the best husbands,
she warned. *Don't be low-hanging fruit!*
Most of us were still playing with dolls,
Mr. Potato Head—using real potatoes—
and watching Popeye cartoons on TV.

Our farm was planted with plum trees
that bore fruit long after my father stopped
farming. I recall scaling a stone-wall
fence covered with poison ivy to pick
the lower branches clean. Damson plums,
purple plums—bursting with sapid sweetness.

The low-hanging fruit always made the best jam.

Joanne Greenway (née Sabarese) was born and raised in a farming community in Ulster County, New York. She holds a Master of Arts in French Literature from Indiana University (1971), but spent the bulk of her working life in the social services field with the Hamilton County Department of Job and Family Services. In 2003, she retired from a 30-year civil service career and finally got around to writing poetry. She joined the Greater Cincinnati Writers League in 2006 and now serves as the organization's president. GCWL recently celebrated the 90th year of its founding with the publication of an anthology, *Within Us*.

Two other chapbooks, *Limited Engagement* and *True Confessions*, were both published by Finishing Line Press, in 2016 and 2019, respectively. Her poems cover a range of subject matter, but childhood memories, loss and aging are the most dominant themes.

In addition to writing, she enjoys reading fiction, biographies and, of course, poetry—and taking full advantage of Cincinnati's rich cultural offerings. Joanne has lived in Cincinnati for fifty years and considers it one of the great nerve centers of poetry in the country. From her perch in the East Price Hill neighborhood, she has an inspiring view of downtown and the mighty Ohio River. Two cats, Lily and Pierre, graciously serve as screen savers when she's trying to write. Both of them are terrible typists.

www.ingramcontent.com/pod-product-compliance
Lightning Source LLC
Chambersburg PA
CBHW020220090426

42734CB00008B/1154